BAITS
for coarse fishing

By Ken Whitehead
Illustrated by Russell Birkett

WARD LOCK

© Text and illustrations Ward Lock Limited 1989

First published in Great Britain in 1989
by Ward Lock Limited, 8 Clifford Street
London W1X 1RB

Designed by Bob Vickers
Text filmset in Times
by Litho Link Ltd, Welshpool, Powys

Printed and bound in Great Britain

British Library Cataloguing in Publication Data
Whitehead, Ken, *1930 Aug. 10 —*
    Baits for coarse fishing. — (Fishing skills
    pocket books).
    1. Coarse fish. Angling
    I. Title II. Series
    799.1′1

ISBN 0-7063-6826-6

CONTENTS

PREFACE

Angling receives a constant flow of newcomers to the sport who must at their introduction face a bewildering complex not only of the 'tools of the trade', the rods, reels, hooks, accessories, styles and so on, but the apparently endless list of baits constantly discussed in the columns of angling books and journals.

But the novice need not stagger back, eyes popping and aghast at the array of tackle and baits on display in tackle shops, because this series of small books has been planned to present the newcomer to coarse fishing with an easy introduction to angling's basic needs.

This volume, concerned with angler's coarse-fishing baits, describes and illustrates the majority of offerings that the newcomer to the sport might consider. There are others, of course, as well as many combinations of those described, but as the thinking angler gains more and more experience there will come a desire to take these standard baits and experiment with others.

The author of this series is Ken Whitehead, an all-round angler happy with whatever species is found in the water he happens to be fishing.

His biggest fish is a pike well in excess of 30 lb and he can include carp in the early 20s among the many entries in his fishing diary. Importantly, he has come to feel that while the pike's lifestyle includes the taking of live fish, the use of livebaiting for the purpose of catching them is not for him.

Ken is also a keen game fisherman and regularly seeks sewin and salmon in Wales as well as trout fishing on many of the southern counties reservoirs. He is a lone angler who fishes for pleasure, wary of angling politics and distrustful of complicated fishing tackle and over-talkative anglers.

The artist responsible for the clear, no-nonsense black-and-white drawings in this series is 23-year-old Russell Birkett, a young graduate with a BA(Hons) degree in Graphic Information and Design. The illustrations in this series are his first major contribution to the field of book illustration and he intends to pursue a career in publishing. He lives in Eastbourne, Sussex.

Len Cacutt, general editor of the series, has for 25 years been closely concerned with angling publishing in all its forms, having himself written a number of books, launched an angling newspaper, and compiled and edited angling books, magazines and encyclopedias for the leading publishers.

INTRODUCTION

The angler's fishing baits are items of food that will entice a fish into feeding so that bait and the hook on which it is impaled will finish up in its mouth. No matter how expensive and sensible an angler's outfit of fishing tackle may be and how expertly he fishes it will all be wasted unless the bait that is used actually attracts fish. To do that a bait must be one of several things.

First it must be fresh. Rarely will fish be attracted to something that is offensive, smells, or tastes rotten. This especially applies to natural baits such as worms, deadbaits, freshwater mussels, and so on. This means that great care should be taken when baits are gathered and prepared, when and how they are kept, and during the time that they are carried to the waterside. More anglers fail to catch fish through baits that are bad and unacceptable to fish than through any other possible cause. This is borne out by L-anglers, fishing clumsily and probably breaking all the rules about care, quiet, stealth and so on, and yet catching fish because they happened to have just the right bait at the right place, at the right time.

Secondly, baits must be attractive – and that means visually as well as gastronomically. Remember that once the bait is in the water it has to be seen or smelled by the fish, often when the water is coloured or when the swim being fished is deep and correspondingly dark. It is therefore obvious that without the all-important element of attractiveness in his bait the angler might just as well fish with a bare hook.

There are, of course, other ways of tempting fish other than by using baits. Spinners, plugs, lures of every colour, shape and size, are splendid fish-takers. But this small volume must concentrate on the angler's hook-baits alone, leaving the huge subject of lures for a possible later volume in this series.

Groundbaits are used by the angler to bring fish into the area in which his hookbait is waiting. Like hookbaits, groundbaits must be fresh and attractive – but not of such wholesome quality that the hookbait itself is ignored. Where this is possible, the bait on the hook must always be just that little bit more obvious. As an example, one whole herring used as a legered hookbait stands out among chopped-up pieces of herring thrown loosely around it.

Although groundbaits are normally used in fairly large quantities they still need to be carefully prepared and properly transported to the waterside if they are to be in tip-top condition on the day that they are used. This means that the angler must take his time and carefully plan the assembly of all the materials he will need well in advance.

PREPARING BAITS

Many baits which the angler uses require cooking, especially those of the pasta and seed kinds. It is as well to have your own saucepans for these, and to make sure that you have a strainer to drain unwanted fluid away after boiling. One of the fine-mesh metal types is ideal, capable of dealing with ingredients up to a pound in weight.

Deadbaits can be purchased and stored in advance. Make sure that you have plenty of plastic bags, and that there is room in the freezer for them. It is also better to label each bag with the contents and date of freezing, so keep a supply of freezer labels that are designed to stick despite the cold.

Many natural baits must be kept alive before use, and some are better when bred by the angler – slugs are an example. A very large aquarium is a sensible investment, to be kept in a dark corner, perhaps in the garage. Feed the slugs on lettuce leaves, potato-peelings and so on, and cover with a lid with air-holes to keep them from straying. Even during the depths of winter the 'slug store' will provide good baits and so prove its worth when collecting outside is virtually impossible.

Pike anglers who are committed to livebaiting will obviously think of building a pond in which to keep baits, so avoiding the problem of catching them during the winter months. A better consideration is a large tank, such as a galvanised cattle drinking-trough, plumbed to allow a supply of water to circulate. It can be kept in an outhouse or garage.

KEEPING BAITS

Cereal and seed-type baits are best chilled after preparation and should be kept in the fridge. Light and transparent Tuppaware or similar airtight and watertight containers are ideal for this purpose. Maggots are best kept chilled after purchase, and again plastic boxes are ideal. Some natural baits from the waterside such as swan mussels or caddis larvae, must be kept in an aquarium until the angler leaves home. Then they need to be carried and kept wet in fresh, damp weed, not water. This kind of bait must not be confined in a small space, so they sometimes require larger-than-usual watertight boxes.

CARRYING BAITS

Hook baits are normally carried in plastic boxes, perforated with air holes in the case of maggots or worms both of which require oxygen. Make sure that the boxes you buy are the right shape and size to fit into your bag or box seat. It is better to standardise them than to have a non-matching collection that requires fitting in your tackle-box like a jigsaw puzzle.

Livebaits are best carried in a large plastic box fitted with a close-fitted lid and handle. Those used to carry plaster and other products of the building industry are ideal – a visit to a building site can sometimes pay dividends. They are expensive, but battery-driven aerators are a must if baits are to be kept alive on any but the shortest of journeys.

Groundbaits are usually carried dry to the waterside and then mixed there so that they adopt the taint of the local water. A sizable canvas bucket is perfect for this task both to carry to the waterside and to mix the groundbait in. Always have expendable pieces of towel to wipe your hands on after mixing groundbait and handling hookbaits.

CEREAL BAITS

Bread

- This is an all-round bait that will attract many different species of fish. It is usually used with a light, powdery groundbait. One large loaf will provide sufficient bait for the average day's sport. (1)

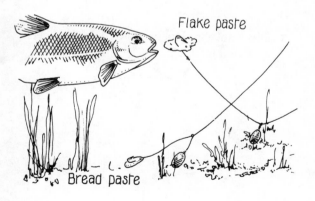

1

Floating crust

Flake paste

Bread paste

Bread Paste

- Remove the soft inside of a loaf at the waterside. (2)

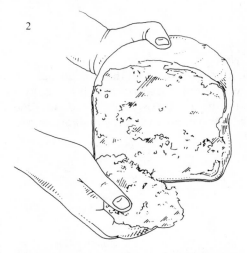

2

- Dip it once into the water and then squeeze it dry immediately. (3).

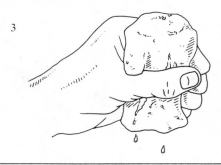

3

- Mould it in a piece of clean, damp rag until it is stiff, and then keep it dry during the day. Pieces can be pulled free and moulded around the hook as required. (4)

4

- Processed cheese, luncheon meat, sausage meat – all these soft products are very attractive to fish and can be moulded into the bait as the paste is made. It is a good way of presenting them. (5, 6)

5

6

- Bread paste can be coloured red, pink, or
  yellow by adding blancmange powder once
  it has been made damp. Colours often
  attract fish when the plain bait fails. (7)

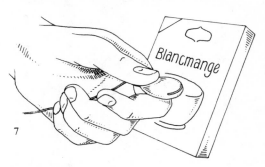

Bread Flake

- Bread flake is made by pulling a piece of
  soft inside from a loaf and moulding it round
  the shank of the hook, leaving the bend and
  point exposed. (8, 9)

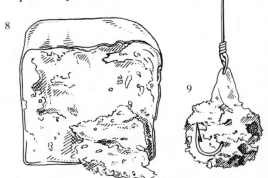

- Naturally, a fresh loaf is best. When not required the loaf should be kept wrapped in a damp cloth to keep it from drying out and going stale.

Floating Crust

- This is a favourite bait for surface-feeding fish such as rudd, chub and carp. It is formed by tearing a piece of crust from a loaf, leaving some soft underside beneath the brown outer surface. Some anglers cut it to form a cube rather than tear an irregular-shaped piece to be mounted on the hook. The shape is of no consequence to the fish. It is important that the crust is soft and not hard, otherwise the hook will break free during the cast. (10)

10

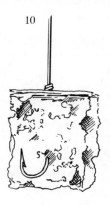

Crust

■ Crust is a sinking type of bait that takes
time to prepare but which is an old and
tested fish-catcher. Start by taking the base
and sides from a square loaf of bread. (11)

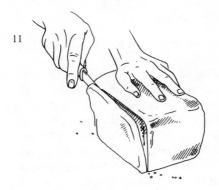

11

■ Wrap it in a damp cloth. (12)

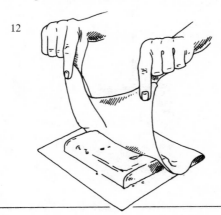

12

■ Place it between two off-cuts of wood. (13)

■ Now put weight on the boards to compress
the crust between them – the leg of a table
often comes in handy! (14)

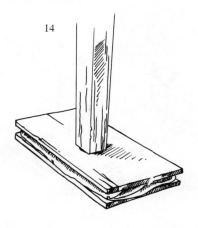

■ Better are two cheap cramps which can be
purchased from a hardware shop and which
will press the bread tightly between the
boards. (15, 16)

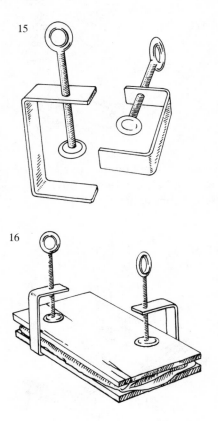

15

16

■ Leave overnight and the next day remove the bread and cut the crust into strips, then into small cubes or triangles, which will move well in the water. Store in a plastic box. (17)

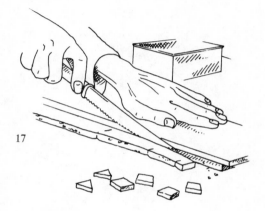

17

Punched Bread

■ A bread punch makes small, hard pellets of soft bread quickly and efficiently. The punch can be purchased at a tackle dealers. and usually comes with several head sizes. (18)

18

- A slice of white bread is put onto a hard surface and the bread punch is pushed hard onto it. (19)

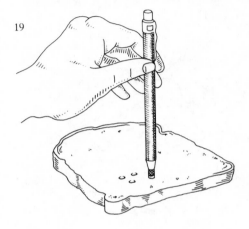

19

- Bait the hook from bread in the punch – don't try to pull the bread free and then put it on the hook.

- Once the hook is into the bread slide it carefully from the punch. An excellent bait for roach fishing, when this species is proving finicky.

Flour Paste

- Another soft hook-bait easily made at home before setting out. Spoon plain flour into a bowl. (20)

20

- Add water and mix until there is a stiff dough and then turn it into a damp rag, or store it in a small plastic box to keep and carry. (21)

21

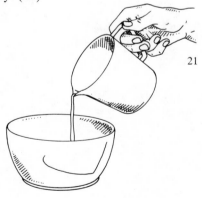

■ Colour and sweetness often add to
attraction – use sugar, blancmange powder
or custard powder for the best results. (22)

22

SEED AND PASTA-TYPE BAITS

Often considered old-fashioned by modern anglers, these are tried and tested favourites that can sometimes be a problem to mount onto a hook. But with perseverance and common sense they can produce results when many other baits fail. (23)

23

Wheat and Pearl Barley

■ Both of these are all-the-year-round baits, with pearl barley often being used as a groundbait to the larger wheat grains. Wheat, also known as creed, used to be more popular than it is today. Prepare them

separately – a pound of either is sufficient
for a day's fishing. (24)

- Cover the grains with water or milk in a
  saucepan and then stew them until the white
  kernel of the grain is just, and *only just*
  showing. (25)

- Avoid over-cooking at all costs – this can make the seed impossible to mount onto a hook. Use a sieve to wash the grains under a cold tap when it is ready, and cold-store in the fridge with a plastic box, taking care to keep the grains moist. Especially in warm weather, keep refrigerated until you are ready to leave home. (26)

26

- Another, easier way to cook wheat and pearl barley is to half-fill a vacuum flask with the grains, filling the remainder of the flask with boiling water. Left overnight, the bait will be ready cooked in the morning –

but remember to cool it once the flask is opened, otherwise the cooking action will continue. (27)

27

Rice

■ Both types of rice, short (or round) and long grained, can be used by the angler. (28)

28

- Long-grained rice is easier to use on the hook, short grained makes groundbait. Tiny though this bait is, it produces excellent results with roach and dace, especially with ultra-fine tackle. Prepare in exactly the same way as wheat and pearl barley but wash in the sieve with hot, not cold water. This will prevent it from lumping. (29)

29

Hempseed

- Good quality hempseed is a winning bait, especially for the match angler. It needs careful preparation if it is to stay on the hook. A pound is normally sufficient for a day. (30)

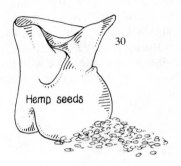

■ Cover the seed with water in a saucepan and bring to the boil. (31)

- Add a teaspoon full of sugar and soda to give sweetness and to intensify the blackness of the seed. (32, 33)

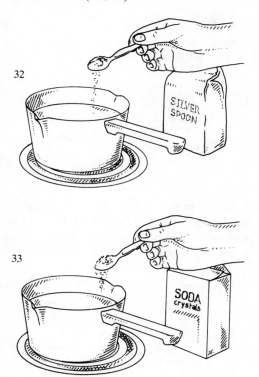

32

33

- Simmer until the white kernel of the seed shows – as for cooking wheat.

- Then take off the heat, sieve and cool with cold water from the tap. (34)

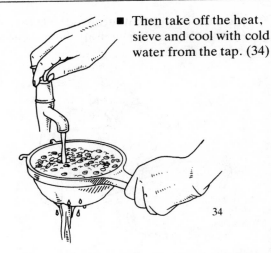

34

- Store the grains, still damp, in an airtight box in the fridge until required. Once at the waterside, dampen the grains again – dried seeds will float and not sink. (35)

35

Sweetcorn

- An expensive but universal bait. It can be used frozen, lightly cooked or straight out of a can. It quickly dries out and should be kept out of direct sunlight on the bank. (36)

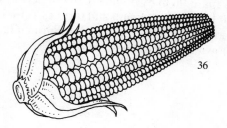

36

- The seeds need to be broadcast over a wide area – a catapult is virtually a necessity for this purpose. One or two seeds on the hook are normal, more if you are legering. (37)

37

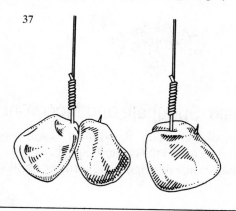

Tares

■ These big seeds – more than twice the size of hempseed – are ideal for use as a hookbait. They are very visible to the fish and are easily mounted on the hook. Prepare them by boiling in the same way as for hemp. Both hemp and tares can also be cooked using the thermos-flask principle shown for wheat preparation. (38)

38

Pasta, Spaghetti and Macaroni

■ Small pasta shells of various sizes will spin and turn with the current. Spaghetti and macaroni will wriggle and turn, worm-like, in the water. All these actions are attractive to fish. (39)

39

Spaghetti

Macaroni

Pasta shells

■ All of these baits should be gently cooked in milk or water until they are soft, then drained and stored in airtight boxes in the fridge until required. (40)

40

■ Both spaghetti and macaroni should be cut
  into small pieces before being mounted
  onto the hook. They are best threaded onto
  the line first, the hook being tied on after
  the bait is in place. (41)

41

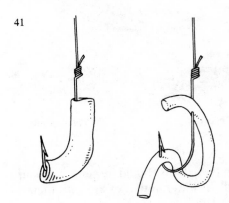

VEGETABLE BAITS

Though alien to fish in their natural
surroundings these baits are often taken by
fish, especially by bottom-feeding species,
though they may take some time to become
educated into accepting them.

Potato

- Universally accepted as a carp bait, the
  potato can be offered in slices, moulded
  from instant mix into balls, or whole, when
  it is par-boiled. (42)

42

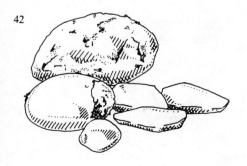

■ Select potatoes in the marble- to golf-ball sizes for par-boiling. New potatoes are especially useful for this. Leave their skins on while cooking takes place, after which they can be scraped using a pan scrub to get smoothness. Boil them long enough to become soft. When they dent under pressure from finger and thumb they are done. Tinned potatoes are ready made for the job – but expensive. (43)

43

■ Potatoes, or pieces of them are mounted
whole on to the hook. Use a baiting needle
to pull line through and then tie the hook
on behind it. Make sure that the point
protrudes. (44)

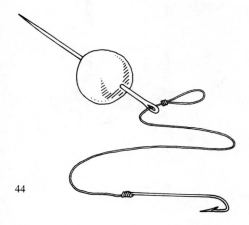

44

Peas

■ An easy bait to mount on the hook, peas
can be frozen, dried or tinned. Various
dried varieties reconstituted and boiled,
using the producer's instructions, make an
excellent groundbait, especially if over-
cooked to the point of being mushy, when
they produce an attractive carpet on the

bottom. Frozen or tinned peas are best for the hook. Remember to keep them moist throughout the day. (45)

45

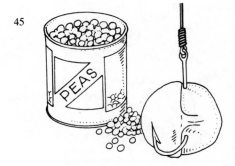

FRUIT BAITS

While many baits we use are completely new to fish, it is possible that they may see at least a few of these. In their natural state fruits are summer specials, but one or two are worth collecting and freezing for use at other times, in combination with other baits.

Blackberries

- A well-proven chub bait where bushes overhang the water. Choose well-ripened fruit, freshly gathered. Free-cast a few berries before offering the fish the berry in which the hook is concealed. The variety known as dew berries, where each fruit segment is twice the normal size, is extra-soft and juicy and well worth the trouble of looking for as the hook bait. (46)

46

Elderberries and Blackcurrants

■ Both elderberries and blackcurrants are
useful baits on their own. But their main
attraction comes when combined with
hempseed. The extra size over that of a
single hemp grain mounted on to a hook,
the ease with which it is mounted and the
jet-black appearance will bring a more
steady, determined bite from fish that often
snatch at free-falling grains. Both berries
are worth gathering in season and
preserving or freezing for use during the
winter. (47)

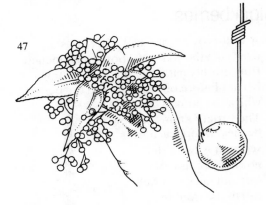

47

Cherries

■ Cherries are another bait associated with
chub, but which have accounted for both
tench and carp. They were first used as a
seasonal bait at Thames weirs, freelined
into the water beside the lasher. Fresh
cherries must be carefully stoned and then
mounted onto a very fine treble hook, the
edges being folded over and pushed through
the soft fruit until the points of the hook
show. Cocktail cherries and cherries used in
confectionery cooking are excellent, besides
being ready for mounting onto a hook. But
it is cheaper to use the natural fruit as free-
offered groundbait. (48)

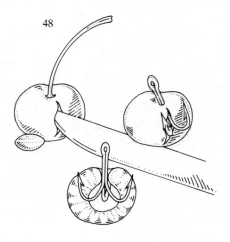

48

Banana

■ Another of the off-beat baits that sometimes
turns up trumps. Worked into bread paste,
with honey or treacle added, the result can
be irresistible to carp. Its softness, however,
makes banana difficult to cast on its own,
and even when combined with a stiffening
medium it still comes away easily from the
hook. Small cubes can be used when long-
trotting, providing that no long-distance
casting has to be undertaken. (49)

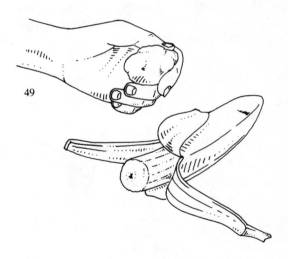

49

CHEESE

Appearance, flavour and ease of presentation make this an all-round bait that has accounted for fish of every variety – even sizable pike. Too much emphasis cannot be laid on the fact that any kind of cheese selected and used must be fresh. (50)

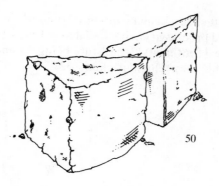

50

■ Hard cheeses can be cut into cubes, triangles or oblongs (the shape encourages movement in the current) and these can be mounted onto the hook making sure that the point of the hook always shows through.

Vary the size of the shapes – cheese cubes tend to float slightly and bigger pieces can help long-trotting tactics. (51)

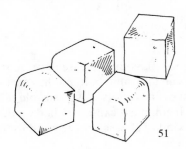

51

■ Soft cheeses can be mounted onto the hook and processed cheeses, sealed in foil, are ideal for this style, moisture being retained while they remain packed. (52)

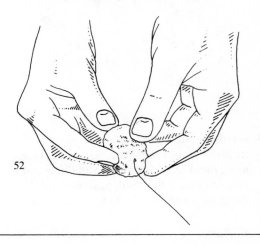

52

■ Hard cheeses can be moulded after being grated with a kitchen grater and then added to bread paste. This method is especially useful when some of the more 'smelly' varieties of cheeses such as Danish Blue and Stilton are being considered. (53)

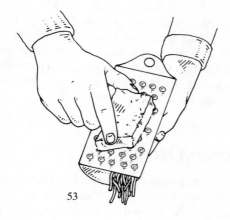

53

MEAT BAITS

These are baits full of surprises. Barbel, carp,
bream – all at some time will feed voraciously
on the various meat baits offered to them by
anglers. Presentation is everything when using
solid meat, and you must be prepared to fiddle
with a baiting needle if your bait is going to be
kept on the hook during casting.

Luncheon Meat

- There are a number of varieties of luncheon
  meat, some going under trade names.
  Basically all are compressed and processed
  meat in tins that are easily carried and can
  be opened on the bank. (54)

54

- Remember to have a tin-opener in your tackle-box in case the built-in one breaks. Heat will make the meat soft and greasy, so retain the tins in a fridge overnight and keep them cool during the day. The cooler the bait is kept, the easier it is to cut into cubes.

- It is worth the trouble of carrying a cutting board and sharp knife with which to cut the meat baits. Cubes are easiest, and once cut, put the pieces back into the tin to help keep them grease-free and solid. (55)

55

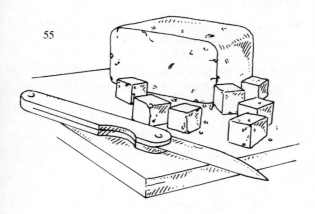

- Use a baiting needle to pass the line through the bait, pulling the hook up against the meat. Take care not to pull the hook too tightly into the cube otherwise you will pad the point and possibly prevent it driving home. (56)

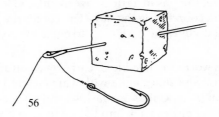

Corned beef

■ Again, a meat bait that lends itself to being cubed and threaded onto the hook. But its coarse texture means that it doesn't remain attached for long once it is under water. Better to crumble it and then work it into a base of bread paste. (57)

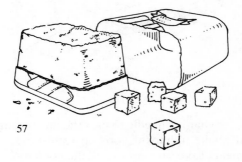

Sausage

■ Sausage meat, as opposed to sausages, makes an excellent additive to paste for the hook. It also works easily into a solid kind of groundbait. Some anglers have had success by working the meat into cubes or balls, then lightly frying them. The treatment serves to keep the bait on the hook. (58)

58

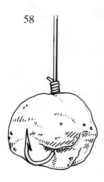

Bacon Fat and Rind

■ Like all meat baits, bacon is unpredictable so far as results are concerned. Strips of fat and short lengths of rind, hooked at one end and long-trotted with a float, will work, worm-like, in the water and can be very effective. The bait is largely and successfully

used in the US; one of the ways in which it
is presented by American anglers is by being
attached to the treble hook on a spinner or
plug and allowed to trail behind the lure
during a retrieve. (59)

59

HIGH-PROTEIN BAITS

Better purchased in powder form from your tackle shop, high-protein (or HP) baits contain casein (milk protein) and the vitamin B complex found in yeast. These are soluble in water. (60)

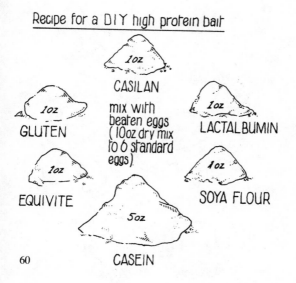

Recipe for a DIY high protein bait

1oz CASILAN

mix with beaten eggs (10oz dry mix to 6 standard eggs).

1oz GLUTEN

1oz LACTALBUMIN

1oz EQUIVITE

1oz SOYA FLOUR

5oz CASEIN

60

■ HP baits can be prepared at home, starting with half a dozen eggs added to a mixture of wheatgerm, soya flour, yeast and casein. Mix the eggs and powder (home-prepared or shop bought) into a paste. Break into small balls and then boil these for a minute or so, until the outer skin toughens. It is possible to add smell to the bait by mixing in gravy powder, Marmite and so on, during the preparation. The whole concept of using HP baits is open to experiment and imagination. (61, 62)

61

62

■ Another method of HP presentation is to mix the ingredients together and then to deep-freeze them uncooked. Carried to the waterside in a vacuum flask, the frozen baits can easily be added to the hook and cast out. But once in the water the bait will melt, becoming soft and allowing its flavour to spread into the surrounding water.

NATURAL BAITS

Free for the taking, and completely acceptable to every species of fish, predators and browsers, natural baits should be high on the angler's menu card. But you need to know when and where to search for them, as well as how they are best kept, if you are going to be sure of an adequate and continual supply. (63)

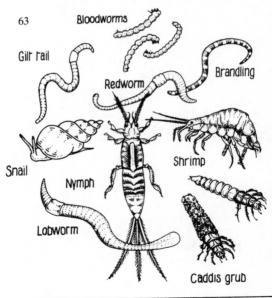

63

Bloodworms

Gilt tail

Redworm

Brandling

Snail

Shrimp

Nymph

Lobworm

Caddis grub

Caddis Larvae

■ Caddis grubs are present in many waters in the British Isles, both still and moving. They carry their own home with them in the form of a tube attached to the body, formed out of local materials which not only give protection, but act as camouflage. They attach themselves to water weed and this is one way of catching them – pulling or raking the weed out and then searching for the grubs. (64)

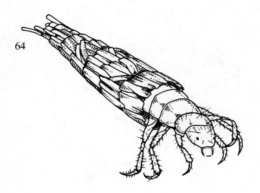

64

■ Another way to obtain grubs is by sinking weighted bunches of twigs into the water, or by suspending cabbage or brussels stumps overnight, collecting them the next day when the caddis larvae will have taken up residence. Never attempt to carry the grubs in water – lack of oxygen will quickly kill

them. Instead, choose a large airtight plastic
box and line the inside of this with wet weed
before turning the grubs into it. Transported
this way, they will keep for 12 hours or so.

■ When placing the grubs onto the hook
  remove the protective casing first, then
  lightly nick the point through the last
  segment of the body, leaving the head free.
  (65, 66)

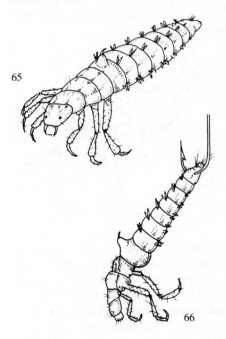

65

66

Caterpillars

- A natural bait where bushes and trees overhang the water, caterpillars can easily be collected from the vegetable garden during the early summer months and kept in an aquarium with a supply of food until required. Lightly hooked through the skin and then dapped (fished in a breeze with an unweighted line) at a rod's length from the bank onto the surface of the water, they are irresistible to chub and rudd. (67)

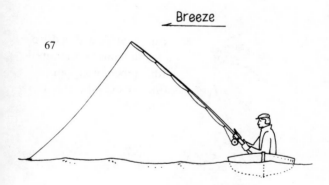

Breeze

67

Crayfish

- This crustacean is found in clear, pure, running water throughout most of the British Isles. The freshwater crayfish looks and behaves exactly like its saltwater relative. (68)

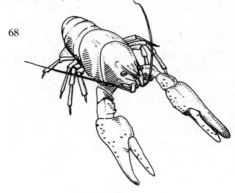

68

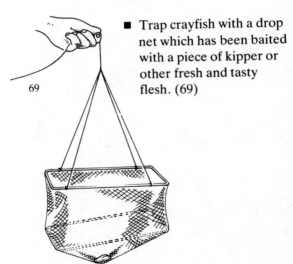

69

- Trap crayfish with a drop net which has been baited with a piece of kipper or other fresh and tasty flesh. (69)

- Evening and early night is the best time for action. Drop the net and leave for several minutes, then raise steadily.

- Don't attempt to carry crayfish in water – instead use the wet weed method, as for caddis larvae.

- Tiny baits are best, mounted whole on a single hook. (70)

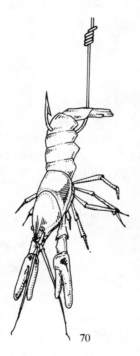

70

■ The tail section, broken from a freshly killed crayfish, is another killing hookbait. But this method demands a large hook. (71)

71

Grasshoppers

■ Easily gathered, grasshoppers should be kept in a small plastic bottle with air holes bored in its lid. From this they can be released one at a time. (72)

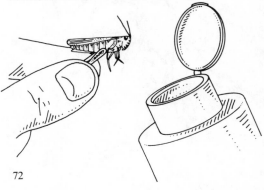

72

■ Mounted on a single hook
  they can be freelined and
  fished on the surface
  or allowed to swim
  in the stream.
  (73)

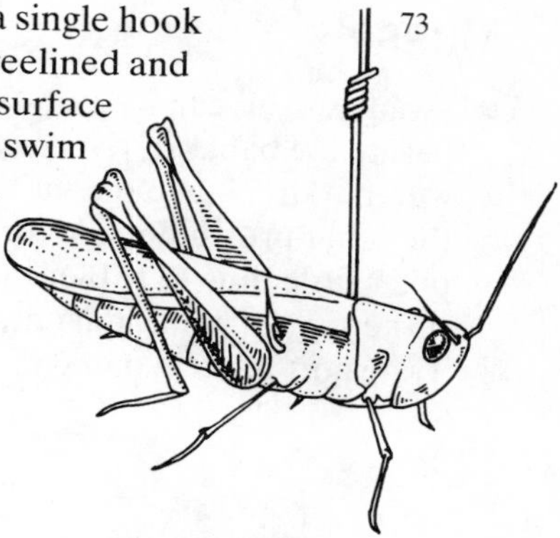

Leeches

■ Horse leeches are an excellent
  bait for bottom feeding fish –
  especially tench and carp.
  They can be sifted from
  mud on the bottom of
  the water and kept in an
  aquarium until required.
  Mount two or more at a
  time on a thin wire hook. (74)

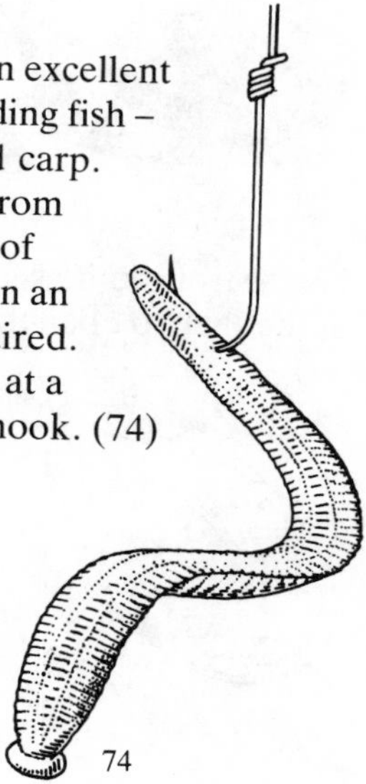

Mussels

■ Swan mussels can be found in shallow water beside the banks of rivers and enclosed waters. They stand on one end in the mud the other protruding out into the water. It takes little time to gather them. They can be kept in an aquarium until required. Transport them in damp moss. (75)

75

■ Use a strong knife slid into the hinged back of the shell to open the mussel. (76)

76

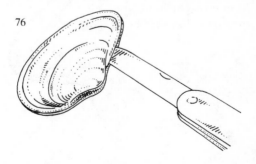

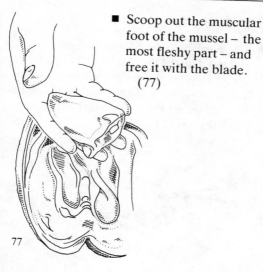

- Scoop out the muscular foot of the mussel – the most fleshy part – and free it with the blade. (77)

77

- Mount the bait onto a large hook, using the shells ground up and added to groundbait as an additional attractor. (78)

78

Shrimps

■ These small freshwater hoppers can be
collected out of the thick blanket weed that
proliferates in many waters. Larger shrimps
can be mounted onto a small, fine wire hook
and are especially killing when allowed to
swim the stream. (79)

79

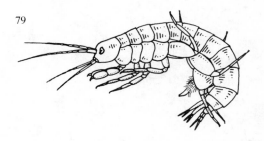

Silkweed

■ A traditional weir bait, where the fine green
strands grow in flowing water on any of the
fixtures and fittings just below the water
level. Rub the weed free with a knife or the
rim of a landing net and don't attempt to
pull it away. Crushing will spoil its
attractiveness and kill the small natural

insects in the weed that fish are looking for.
(80)

80

■ Keep the weed in water, in a plastic box.
Bait the hook by drawing it through the
weed and allowing it to catch to the shank
of the hook. Don't squeeze or twist it on.
Some anglers use a tiny triangle which baits
more easily. (81)

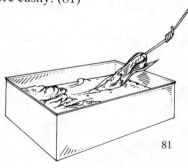

81

- Swim the stream using a big float that can be seen. Keep a tight line which will allow you to feel, as well as see a take. (82)

82

Slugs

- Once a supply of slugs have been gathered from the garden they can be kept in a moist aquarium, fed, and allowed to breed. This will give a supply of baits for a large part of the year. All colours of slug, red, black, and grey, are acceptable to fish, especially chub. (83)

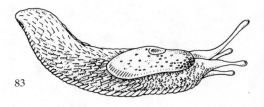

83

- Take a supply to the waterside with a few lettuce leaves, contained in a plastic drum with a handle that can be attached to your belt. Also carry a large, old towel with which to clean your hands – slugs are sticky and slimy. Use a large (size 4) hook and impale the slug through the body. (84)

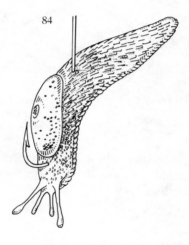

84

- Freeline slugs, casting well upstream into weed and allowing the bait to work back on the stream, keeping a tight line. Chub especially will take this bait with considerable force.

Snails

■ Ram's horn, pond and river snails are the bigger species that can be found feeding in weed clumps, and which make an excellent bait. Keep in an aquarium and carry in wet weed. (85)

85

■ The hard shell is best crushed before mounted onto a hook. This will allow easy mounting.

Worms

■ Everyone's idea of a fishing bait, whether an angler or not. Worms account for more fish during a year than any other bait – and will catch every species of fish. But catching and keeping worms is as important as fishing with them, especially if the angler wants the worms to be available during summer when drought drives them deep underground or winter's cold keeps them from view.

■ There are three main species of worm that are useful to the angler, they are the lobworm, redworm and brandling. Lobworms are by far the biggest in size and can be identified by the large thick circle that runs around the body. Redworms are smaller, up to 4 in long, while brandlings, similar in size to the redworm, can be identified by a series of yellow rings that encircle the red body. (86)

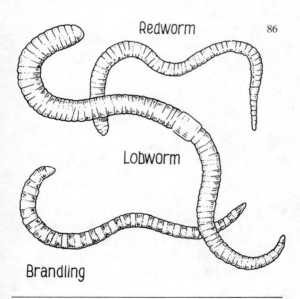

Redworm   86

Lobworm

Brandling

■ Lobworms can be gathered from a lawn
after dark, when they come to the surface.
In dry weather a good watering helps to
bring them up. The other two worm species
are usually found in manure heaps or under
stones and rotted branches on the ground.
Once gathered, keep the worms in
sphagnum moss (you can buy it at a florist)
which is dampened down. Examine the
worms each day and remove the dead ones,
their presence quickly kills all the others.
(87)

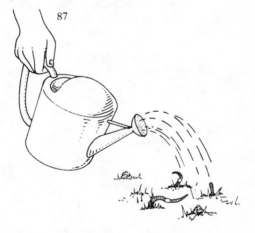

87

■ It is easy to make a wormery of your own.
Sink a large wooden box in a corner of the
garden, make a few holes in the bottom for
drainage and then fill this with soil and, if
available, dead leaves and a little garden

refuse. Water it, place your worms on the soil and then cover completely with old, wet newspapers or a large plastic bag. Even in a heavy frost the worms will be ready to dig up.

■ Take care when you impale your worm on the hook. They are quickly stripped during a long cast – especially if a large worm has been put onto a small hook. Don't forget that it is possible to use two hooks, mounted one above the other or even a three-hook rig on which the worms can be fastened, showing them under the water in their full length, not just a jumbled and uninteresting ball. (88)

88

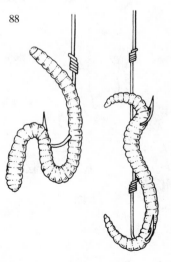

Bloodworms

■ This tiny bait is not a worm at all but the larva of a gnat or midge. It is also known as tubifex and as such is obtained by aquarists as food for their pet fish. Due to the problems of collecting it, the bloodworm is not often on sale as an anglers' bait. The dedicated bloodworm angler will wade in thick mud to scrape the tiny larvae from its surface. (89)

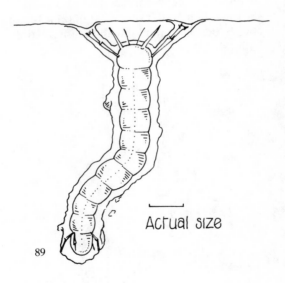

Actual size

89

- Due to their size, hooking bloodworms is not easy, the traditional method being to lay the thin, tiny larva on the ball of the thumb and impale it on a very fine, sharp hook. (90)

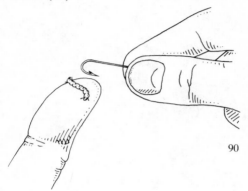

90

Maggots

- Probably the most popular bait used in coarse angling, maggots are best purchased from the tackle shop. It is possible to breed them, but it takes considerable skill and time to produce a really acceptable bait. Maggots for the hook are the larvae of the bluebottles and the largest in size. The greenbottle gives a maggot known as a pinkie, inferior to that of the bluebottle, while the common or garden housefly gives a small maggot known as a squatt, so

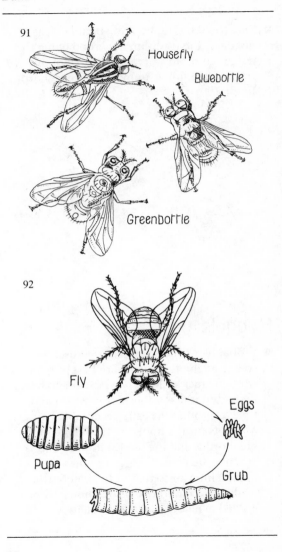

91

Housefly

Bluebottle

Greenbottle

92

Fly

Eggs

Pupa

Grub

insignificant that it generally finishes up with the pinkie being used as groundbait. (91, 92)

■ Maggots that are not kept properly will soon pupate and turn into casters, which are a bait in their own right. Collect maggots from the shop in a ventilated box and immediately store them in the fridge until they are required. Kept like this they will remain motionless and last for several days. Two days before use, sieve them to remove all sawdust and unwanted material in which they may have been packed. There is an excellent purpose-built sieve on the market that will do this. Once separated, turn the maggots out on to fine sand and leave them to work through this for 24 hours while they further cleanse themselves. (93)

93

■ Then sieve the maggots once more, freeing them of sand. Turn them into bran or oatmeal which will polish them and help free them of grease – which causes them to float – and keep them in this until they are used.

- Hook the maggot through the blunt end, where the two black spots are, and not the sharp end. This will allow it to wriggle attractively in the water. (94)

94

Casters

- The dark-coloured caster, which is the chrysalid of the maggot, is a seductive bait that can be bred or purchased from the tackle shop.

- It takes six days for a maggot to turn into a caster. Maggots that are separated and turned out into clean material should be tipped into a tin or box so that they cover the bottom to a depth of an inch or so. Keep them in a cool place and watch them daily. When the first caster appears, turn the maggots into a sieve and allow them to work through and back into their original box. Casters only will be left in the sieve. Repeat this process as often as necessary.

- When sufficient quantities have been separated and collected, drop them into a bowl of water. Those that float have no great use and should be discarded and flushed away. Those remaining should be packed into a plastic bag and stored again in the fridge, ready for use.

- Hook the caster through the end, turning the point and bend so that it lodges in the body of the chrysalid itself. Use a fine-wire hook. (95)

95

Wasp and Docken Grubs

■ The wasp grub is another maggot, of a sort, but a much larger and sweeter grub. It is a traditional countryman's bait that has accounted for many specimen-sized fish. But collecting this grub is a hazardous business and should not be attempted by poking about in a wasp nest! There are chemical methods, but these must only be used after expert advice and then under supervision. As its name implies, the docken grub is found in the roots of that plant. It is a very soft, segmented bait and it is difficult to avoid spoiling it when hooking. Very fine wire hooks are needed, the sharp barb being inserted just nicked into the skin. (96)

96

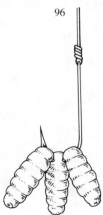

BAIT ADDITIVES

There are a large number of additives that may be mixed with practically any hookbait. We have already discussed the use of blancmange powder, sugar, and soda when we prepared some of the baits described above. There are many more, some good, some indifferent. Many anglers believe that there must be one super-secret additive that will bring every species of fish on to immediate and savage feed. There is no such miracle substance! But there are many additives that bring success when used sensibly and with consideration of the time of year, water and bait. The subject attained a kind of cult image a few years ago, with closely guarded 'secret' formulae being devised.

Various essences used in cooking such as vanilla, almond and so on, are some, aniseed is another, that were thought at one time to be deadly. Bovril, Oxo, Marmite all help, especially with meat-type baits. Honey is yet another tried additive together with treacle. They can bring success to fish with a 'sweet tooth', such as carp. Pilchard oil, oil of geranium, blood from the abattoir – all have

their day. It is up to the angler to experiment
and blend to get the most from what is
available. (97)

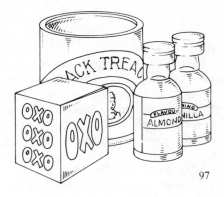

97

COCKTAIL BAITS

Cocktail baits are two or more items gathered on the same hook – virtually a sandwich – which can improve a single attractiveness. There are endless permutations, but a few examples could be a maggot added behind a piece of crust, imparting movement to it as it swims the stream; cheese mounted behind meat – the lightness of the cheese constrasting with the dark of the meat; maggot and caster, again light and dark. When making a cocktail bait aim always to improve the single bait you are using.

GROUNDBAITS

A general rule of thumb for groundbaits is to remember that light, powder-type groundbaits are used for stillwaters and those that are slow flowing. Heavy groundbaits are used in fast flowing waters or those where it is necessary to cast or throw the bait over a distance from the bankside.

- Traditionally, light groundbaits are made from dried bread, ground either in a mincer or pounded into crumbs. Alternatives are biscuits, crumbed down, or some of the commercial products such as sausage rusk, bran, crushed oats. (98)

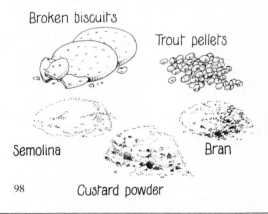

Broken biscuits

Trout pellets

Semolina

Bran

98   Custard powder

- Heavy groundbaits have bread as a base, soaked and then stiffened with the addition of bran, brewers' grains, cattle feed – any bulk substance that will help the bread to be moulded into heavy balls that can be thrown over a distance and which will sink rapidly.

- Groundbaits are best mixed at the waterside and a canvas bucket is ideal for both carrying and mixing in. (99)

99

Maggots

Flour   Sweetcorn

- Many additives can be used to improve the basic groundbait. Examples are legion. The water in which hempseed has been boiled helps to add attraction, as does the seed itself when it has been dried, crushed and mixed into the groundbait base. Potatoes boiled and mashed, then added to a heavy groundbait give an exceptional mix useful for floodwaters and the angler who wishes to use par-boiled potato as bait. Cheese ground with a hand grater and added to the mix, sausage meat, blood, all help to give attraction and to tempt fish close to whatever hookbait the angler may be using.

■ Finally there are loose groundbaits, basically offerings of the hookbait thrown into the swim or broadcast around it. Small pellets of paste, loose hemp grains, a few cubes of luncheon meat – all advertise the presence of food. But groundbait should never be offered in such quantities that the fish feed on it while the angler's baited hook is overlooked as it lies on the bottom. (100)

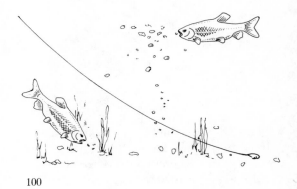

100

INDEX